# Lucas and Emily's Food Bank Adventure

Written by
**Dave Grunenwald**

Illustrated by
**Bonnie Lemaire**

**Halo**
PUBLISHING
INTERNATIONAL

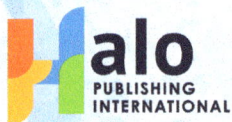

Halo Publishing International
7550 W IH-10 #800, PMB 2069,
San Antonio, TX 78229

First Edition, June 2025
ISBN: 978-1-63765-759-1
Library of Congress Control Number: 2025908431

Halo Publishing International is a hybrid publishing company that works with authors to bring their stories to life. We publish adult fiction and non-fiction, children's books, self-help, spiritual, and faith-based titles.

Have a book idea you'd like us to consider?
Visit www.halopublishing.com to learn more about how we can help you publish and promote your book.

This book is dedicated to grandparents and grandchildren around the world who are sharing their own adventures and working together to help their communities every day.

Continued thanks for their assistance goes to my daughters Jill Grunenwald and Amy Burke, and to my associate, Terry Stephens.

Thanks also to my grandsons L. D. Burke, for his ideas and creativity, and M. B. Burke, for his humor and inspiration.

"How was school today, Lucas?" Grandpa asks.

"It was good. I had music and art."

"Did Mom pack you a lunch?"

"She did, but, Grandpa, my friend Tommy did not have a lunch when we first sat down in the cafeteria, so I offered him half of my sandwich."

"That was nice of you, Lucas!" says Grandpa.

Lucas adds, "He said thank you, but he didn't take it because the school had a lunch ready for him, and he just had to walk over to get it."

"Why do some people need food?" asks Lucas. "I thought everyone had food."

"Lucas, there are many people who don't have enough food at home. They just need a little extra help to get some. You know how your dad has a job?" Grandpa asks. "Well, some people do not have jobs."

He then explains, "When someone does not have a job, they don't earn money, and without money, it's hard to buy food or the other things they need to live."

After a moment's thought, Grandpa says, "Lucas, I have an idea."

"What's that?" Lucas asks.

"I have some friends who make lunches for people who need food. We could visit them today," answers Grandpa.

"That would be great, Grandpa. Can Emily come along?"

"Of course! Jack can come too."

Lucas runs excitedly to share the news with his friends. A few moments later, Emily and Jack arrive, and they all pile in the car and get on their way.

As they pull into the parking lot, Grandpa says, "Today is the day of the week they pack lunches here for people who are homeless."

"Homeless?" asks Lucas.

"Yes, Lucas, some people do not have a permanent place to live, so they might live, for example, in a tent at the local park or other places," Grandpa explains.

He adds, "These folks who pack lunches for them are known as the Sandwich People."

"Sandwich People?" Lucas and Emily say as they look at each other quizzically.

Hopping out of the car, they all approach the front door and are greeted by Cathy and Jerry, the volunteer coordinators.

"Hello, Grandpa. Hello, kids!" Cathy says.

"So the Sandwich People are just people! They aren't giant sandwiches with legs!" whispers Lucas to Emily as they head to the community room where people are preparing bagged lunches.

Emily giggles.

They are greeted by some of the volunteers.

"Hello, kids! Do you want to help?"

"Yes!" both Lucas and Emily say enthusiastically.

"Me too!" says Jack.

14

There are two tables lined with food items. Volunteers are taking turns and filling lunch bags down each aisle.

"Grab a bag, move down the aisle, and place one of each item in the bag," Cathy explains. "We have such things as fruit drinks, fruit bars, chips, and applesauce."

"How about a sandwich?" asks Emily.

"We add those later," answers Cathy.

"How often do you do this?" asks Lucas.

"Once a week," Cathy answers.

"I'm so happy Grandpa brought us in to help today! Maybe he can bring us again next week," Lucas says.

"I liked learning how the Sandwich People put together lunch bags for those in need," says Lucas.

"It's a wonderful thing to do because so many people rely on the help of others to obtain food," Grandpa responds.

"Are there other places that help people like that?" Emily asks.

"Yes, there are. Another example is the food bank. Would you like to visit one?" Grandpa asks.

"Yes," the kids respond.

"What's a food bank?" asks Lucas as they head to the car.

BE A NEIGHBORHOOD **HERO** and help SUPPORT your LOCAL FOOD BANK!

FOOD BANK

OPEN

Arriving at the food bank, Grandpa points and says, "That is a food bank."

"It's ginormous," says Lucas.

"Lucas, Denny works here, and he will tell you all about the food bank," says Grandpa.

When they all get to the front door, they are greeted by Denny.

"Welcome to the food bank," Denny says enthusiastically. "Would you like a tour?"

Lucas and Emily both shout, "Yes!" and they all head inside.

COMMUNITY
FOOD BANK

"This is the storage room," Denny explains as the kids look in amazement at all the racks of food.

"Many people and companies in town donate food, and this is where we store it," says Denny. Then he adds, "Others donate money so we can buy more."

Jack looks up and says, "Big."

"That's a lot of food," says Emily. Then she asks, "Why do you have so much?"

"We distribute food to nearly half a million people a year."

"This is the packing room," says Denny. "This is where we bag and box food for delivery to people or for them to pick up."

"Whom do you deliver food to?" asks Lucas.

"Some people cannot pick up food because they may be homebound or do not have a car," Denny answers. "In that case, we deliver it to where they live."

"Homebound?" asks Lucas with a puzzled look.

"Some people cannot drive because they may be, for instance, in a wheelchair or cannot walk. In those cases, we deliver the food to them," Denny explains.

"Why do you volunteer to pack food?" Emily asks a young volunteer.

Looking around and pointing, the volunteer replies, "We all give our time because many, many people need food, and we simply want to help."

"That is very good of you," says Lucas.

"Food banks, big and small, all across the country, depend on volunteers," says Denny.

"We all depend very much on those who contribute money and food, and the volunteers who make it happen," he adds.

"There are dozens of food banks in the area and thousands across the country," Denny explains. "Food banks are large and small."

"How many people get their food from a food bank?" asks Grandpa.

"Well, all over the country, millions," Denny answers.

"That's a lot," says Emily.

"Lucas, would you like to visit a small food bank?" asks Grandpa.

"Yes."

"Then let's go."

Grandpa pulls the car into the parking lot of a local food bank. It looks like the big one in the city, only smaller.

Entering the building, they begin to look around.

"Would you like a tour?" asks Joan, a volunteer who greets them just inside the door.

"We just left the food bank in the city and wanted to visit a local one," Grandpa says.

"Great," says Joan as she explains they do everything the food bank in the city does, just on a smaller scale.

Pointing to a room with people in it, Lucas asks, "Are those volunteers?"

"Yes," Joan answers, adding, "most of our volunteers live nearby."

"Would you like to help pack boxes?" asks one of the volunteers.

"That would be great. We would love to help!" says Emily.

After a bit of instruction, the kids all pitch in, even Jack. He hands items to both Lucas and Emily.

"I never was a volunteer before," says Lucas. "This is fun!"

"We enjoy volunteering and are glad to help those in need," says Joan, adding that her mom and brother are also volunteering that day. "It's a family tradition!"

Joan explains, "We have one more thing to do."

"What's that?" asks Emily.

"We need to load the boxes into a van so they can be delivered to those who need the food," she replies.

"Can we help?" asks Lucas.

"Help," says Jack.

"Yes, of course," answers Joan.

The kids take turns helping to load boxes into the van. When finished, they jump in the car to head home.

"We are among the lucky ones, kids," says Grandpa. "Our families have the money to buy food and clothes and take care of our needs."

He further states, "Not everyone is so fortunate."

"I am glad there are food banks," says Lucas.

"Me too," says Emily.

"There are also book banks and clothing banks that provide books and clothing for those in need," Grandpa says.

"Grandpa, can we visit a book bank someday?" asks Lucas.

"Absolutely!" says Grandpa.

*To be continued...*

For more information, visit
www.grandparentmeritbadges.com,
its related blog, and its Facebook page.
As we like to say:

**DISCONNECT FROM THE DIGITAL™**
**AND**
**RECONNECT WITH THOSE WHO MATTER MOST**

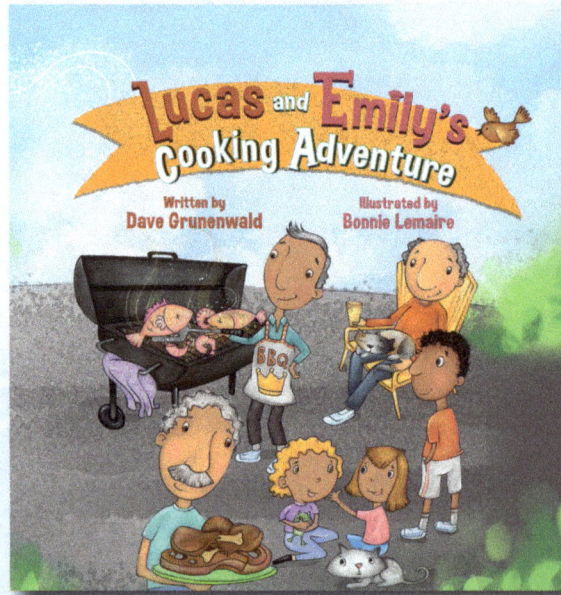

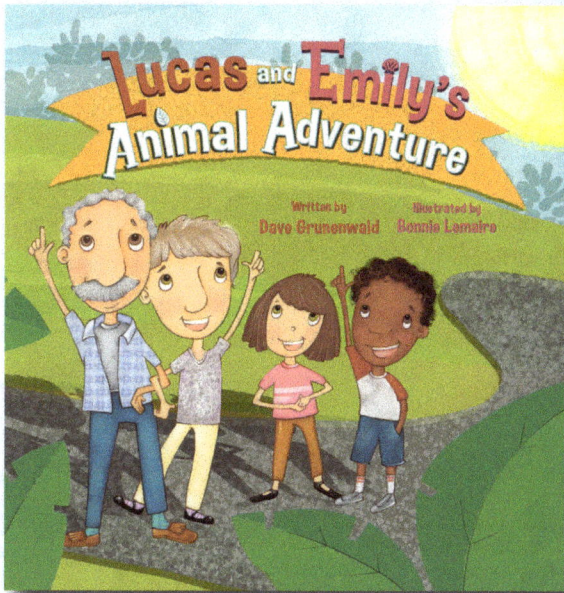

Lucas and Emily's
Animal Adventure

Written by
Dave Grunenwald

Illustrated by
Bonnie Lemaire

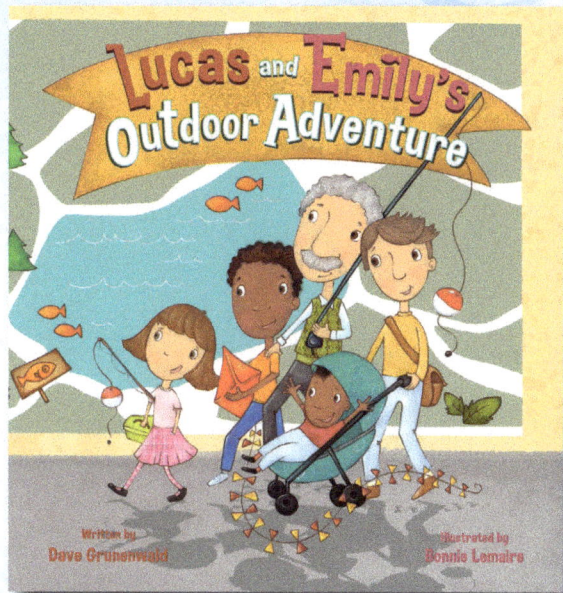

Lucas and Emily's
Outdoor Adventure

Written by
Dave Grunenwald

Illustrated by
Bonnie Lemaire

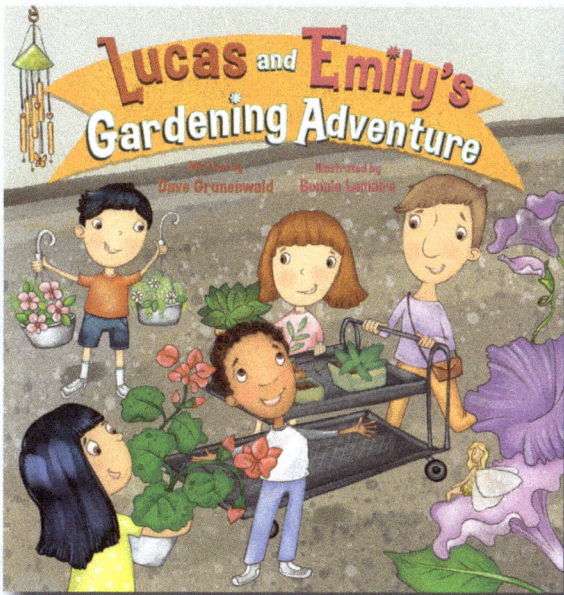

Lucas and Emily's
Gardening Adventure

Written by
Dave Grunenwald

Illustrated by
Bonnie Lemaire

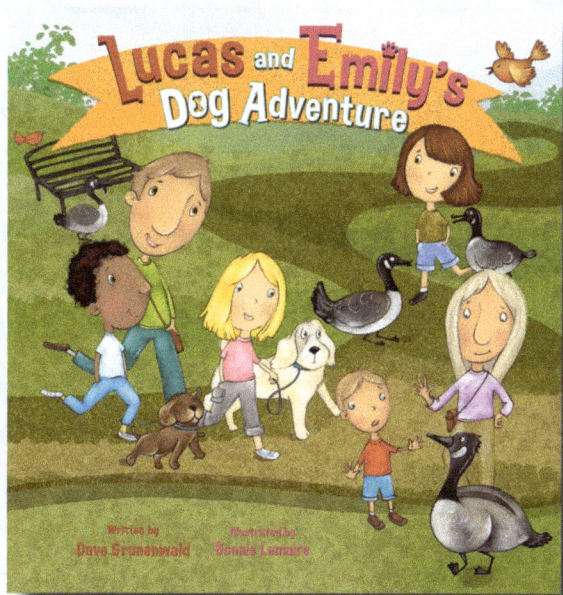

Lucas and Emily's
Dog Adventure

Written by
Dave Grunenwald

Illustrated by
Bonnie Lemaire